WOODLORE

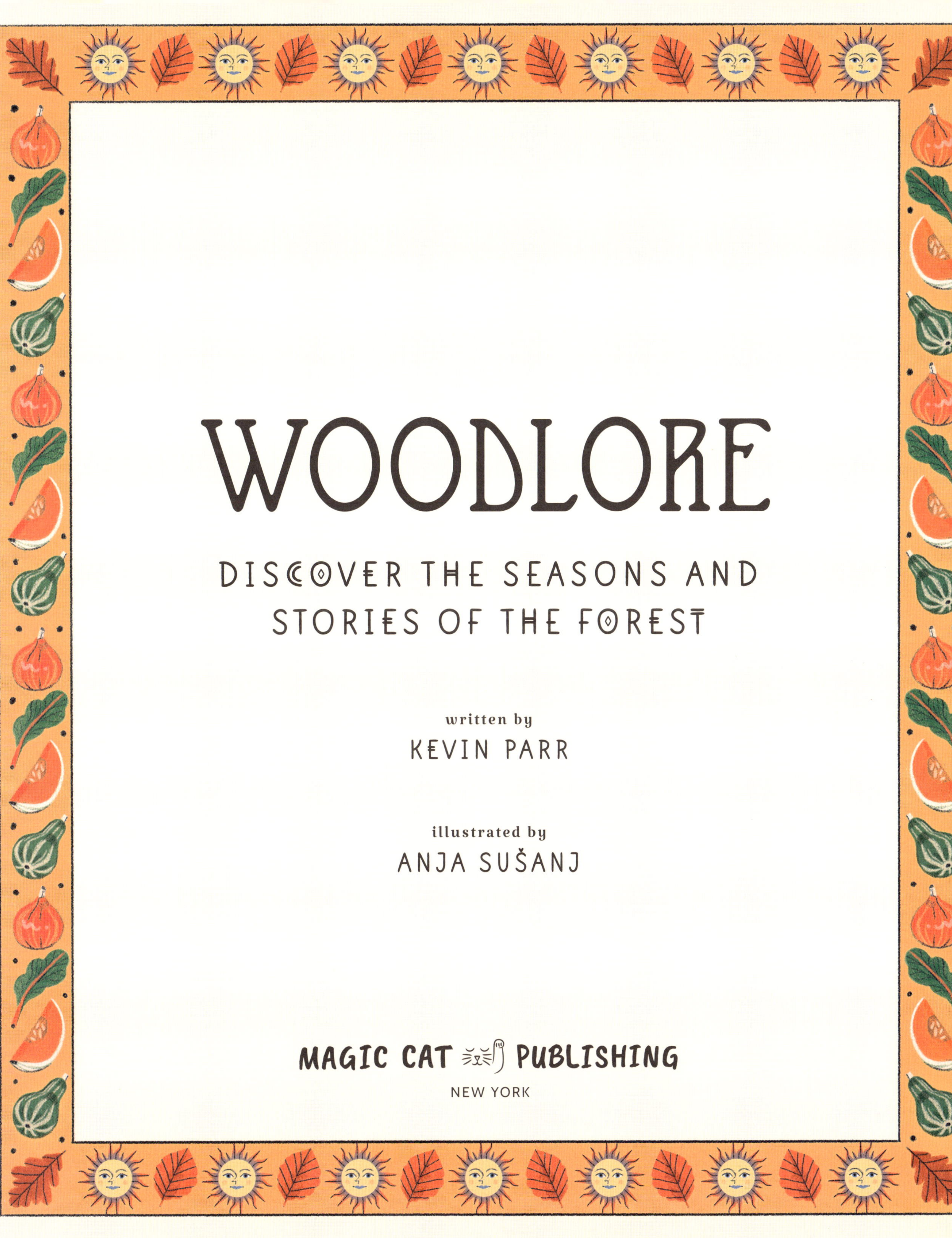

WOODLORE

DISCOVER THE SEASONS AND STORIES OF THE FOREST

written by
KEVIN PARR

illustrated by
ANJA SUŠANJ

MAGIC CAT PUBLISHING
NEW YORK

FOREWORD

A woodland stirs to the rhythm of the year, with subtle changes that breeze through every season. From the vibrancy of spring to the sullen reflection of autumn, the moods of the forest often echo our own lives.

Since the dawn of time, people have lived and worked with trees in a relationship of give and take. Ancient mythology and timeless traditions mark the turning of the year, from the summer solstice, when we celebrate the longest day, to the winter solstice, when we wassail, or wish each other well, during the longest night.

Woodlore celebrates all forest life, from the buzz of bumblebees and the bellow of bears to the mysterious mushrooms and flowers within which fairies are said to shelter.

So, join us among the trees, and let's uncover some of their stories and secrets.

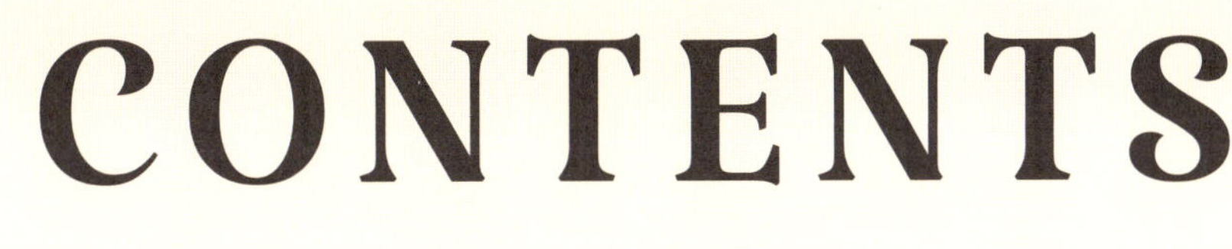

6 ◊ AN OAK

SPRING

8 ◊ The Spring Equinox

10 ◊ Understory in Spring

12 ◊ Woodland Flowers

14 ◊ Nests & Burrows

SUMMER

16 ◊ The Summer Solstice

18 ◊ Butterflies & Moths

20 ◊ Fledglings

21 ◊ Bats

22 ◊ Gall Ink

24 ◊ Green Man

AUTUMN

26 ◊ The Autumn Equinox

28 ◊ A Buzz in the Woodland

30 ◊ Fungi

32 ◊ Berries, Nuts & Hips

34 ◊ Owls

WINTER

36 ◊ The Winter Solstice

38 ◊ Mistletoe

40 ◊ Hibernation

42 ◊ Tree Blessings

44 ◊ Winter Woodlore

AN OAK

I feel small when I walk among the trees.

Not just because they are bigger than me, but because they are often much older and have so many stories to share. Sometimes it is nice to feel small.

The first trees appeared nearly four hundred million years ago, long before the first people, and there are trees alive today that may be as old as the pyramids in Egypt.

Trees and woodlands are deeply entwined within folklore and can mean different things to different peoples.

They are incredible habitats for wildlife, too—of all shapes and sizes.

A single oak tree can support more than two thousand other species, including birds, mammals, and insects. Just imagine what you might find in a whole forest!

In North America, some common species include the white oak, pin oak, black oak, and live oak.

All oak trees experience changes as the seasons unfold. Let's visit one tree across the seasons and watch it transform.

What Oaks Share

There are more than five hundred species of oak across the world—from the Hungarian oak in Europe to the Chinese cork oak in Asia. Yet wherever they grow, they are all part of the same family and same genus. The oak tree's Latin name is *Quercus*.

THE SPRING EQUINOX

Let's begin our woodland journey in spring.

The cold and dark of winter finally give way to lighter and longer days, until finally, daytime and nighttime are of exactly equal length. This moment of perfect balance is known as the spring equinox, a date celebrated around the world as a time of beginnings and renewal.

Our oak tree, too, comes into bud in spring. Meanwhile, little acorns take root, beginning their epic journey that will stretch far into the future: It is said that an oak tree grows for three hundred years, lives for three hundred years, and then dies for three hundred years. Some oak trees may live for more than one thousand years. Their long life is one reason why they are associated with fertility, health, and fortune.

Beltane

In European folklore, oak would be used to make a drill that would be spun against a flat piece of wood until it caught fire.

This was called a needfire and would be lit at the festival of Beltane (a May Day celebration), whereafter the ashes would be mixed with seeds to protect them and bring healthy growth to the crops.

male flowers

Silver Clouds

Almost all kinds of oak are deciduous, which means that they begin the year without any leaves.

The oak is monoecious, which means that both male and female flowers grow on the same tree. Some trees, such as the yew, are dioecious, meaning that male and female flowers grow on different trees.

The male flowers grow first and they appear just before the leaves begin to unfurl, forming small bunches on thin green stems. The female flowers are harder to spot, appearing as small, red buds. They appear once the male flowers mature and turn golden, and as the wind blows, pollen from the male flowers rides the breeze and attaches to the female flowers. Sometimes, on a warm spring day, you might see clouds of pollen released from trees with every gust of wind.

female flowers

Understory in Spring

The forest branches above remain bare, but life stirs in the undergrowth below . . .

Before the leaves of deciduous trees form a thick, woodland canopy and block out much of the light, lots of smaller plants make the most of the spring sunshine. These flowers, bushes, and small trees form what is known as the understory.

Shade

Because understory species cannot compete with the taller trees for height, they grow more densely and are often tightly packed to the forest floor. This means that they create lots of additional shade, which helps to retain moisture and maintain a steady temperature.

Protection

The understory offers vital cover for animals and birds, while invertebrates are drawn by the thick carpet of lichen and moss. It also helps protect the roots and trunk bases of the larger trees, which in turn protect the smaller species from extremes of weather.

Saplings

Within the understory, young saplings of trees like beech and ash wait to one day grow tall and become a part of the canopy. The saplings require less moisture and sunlight than the older trees and can survive at a stunted height until one of the bigger trees dies or gets toppled in a storm, at which point the saplings can grow up and take their place.

Evergreens

Other trees are specialists of the understory. They might be evergreen species, such as the holly, which means their leaves can soak up any sunlight that shines through the winter.

In Norse mythology, holly was associated with Thor, the god of thunder, and trees were often planted near homes to protect them from lightning.

Dogwood

Dogwood is another deciduous understory tree that can be spotted in winter due to the red color of fresh twig growth. Dogwood thrives in shady, damp conditions, so is perfect in the understory. Its wood is incredibly hard and has traditionally been used to make crucifixes, and it bursts into flower each spring.

In Christian legend, **dogwood** was used to make the cross on which Jesus was crucified, and one species, the flowering dogwood, native to North America, has petals that form a cross with notches that are said to resemble the indentations of the crucifixion nails.

Woodland Flowers

A woodland floor can glow with color in early spring.

First comes the green of stalks and leaves, inching skyward before winter has left. These are plants hardened against late snowfall and frost because they have to soak up as much sunshine as they can before the canopy closes above them. And after the gray of winter, the flowers that follow float among the green like fallen jewels, providing vital food for buzzing bees and other pollinating insects.

Bluebells form vast, shimmering carpets of mauve-blue in late spring. They have a long association with faerie folk, and it is said that should you pick one, a fairy might whisk you away and lead you astray!

Lesser Celandine

The yellow of the lesser celandine is rich and golden like the sun. They were the favorite flower of the poet William Wordsworth, who wrote:

"And, the first moment that the sun may shine,
Bright as the sun himself, 'tis out again!"

I always smile when I find the first one of the year, it reminds me that spring is coming, bringing life and warmth with it.

The wood anemone is crisp and white and also known as a windflower, which is a translation from the Greek for "anemone."

They are a slow-growing plant, so only appear in large numbers in ancient forests. The petals close when it rains, and it was once believed that fairies would hide inside to shelter from a downpour.

Bloodroot is similar in appearance to the wood anemone but grows in North America, where it prefers a dry woodland habitat. It is named after the red or orange toxic sap it produces, which indigenous tribes of eastern North America, including the Algonquin, Iroquois, and Sioux, used to cure ailments and as a natural dye.

Something Old

Some birds will use the same nest as the previous year, but will tidy it up and make necessary repairs. The osprey will use the same site year after year and generation after generation. An old nest might be more than 6 feet (2 m) across and as deep as 13 feet (4 m)!

Something New

A lot of birds will build a new nest each spring. Long-tailed tits make enclosed nests from moss that they glue together using spiderwebs.

Nests & Burrows

Lots of animals are busy in spring building nests.

In the branches, mammals such as the gray squirrel build dreys which are made from branches, twigs, and leaves and look a lot like birds' nests. On the forest floor, animals like the badger, red fox, and eastern chipmunk dig burrows underground. These might be a complex maze of tunnels and chambers, often using the roots of trees to provide structure. But the world's best-known nest builders in the forest are the birds, who create all kinds of structures in all shapes and sizes.

Something Borrowed

The peregrine falcon will wait until another bird has finished nesting before moving in.

Something Blue

Wood thrushes build neat bowls with a smooth mud and clay lining, and lay their beautiful blue eggs inside.

Nests Up High

Penduline tits in Eurasia and North Africa hang their nests from slender branches of willow or birch trees and make a small tunnel near the top.

Nests That Buzz

Insects like hornets and bumblebees will build nests in crevices and holes, particularly in older or dead trees.

Nests in Holes

Woodpeckers make holes in tree trunks in which to nest, while birds like the nuthatch nest in natural tree cavities or holes abandoned by woodpeckers.

Nests Down Low

Some bird species, such as the woodcock, will build nests on the ground and rely on camouflage to avoid predators.

THE SUMMER SOLSTICE

The branches and leaves are buzzing with life.

The summer solstice marks the longest day of the year. At the time of the solstice, our oak tree is in full leaf. The leaves grow in small bunches, forming a rich and vibrant shimmer of green, each one lobed and standing stiff on a short stalk.

A single oak tree can support over two thousand other species of insects, plants, lichens, fungi, mammals, and birds, some of which are not found on any other tree. Butterflies and moths flutter among its branches, while fledgling birds and bats take cover in its thick canopy of leaves.

Sacred Trees

For so long, trees have been worshipped and held in high regard. They provide us with food, fuel, and shelter, and even produce oxygen through photosynthesis, which helps us breathe. So many cultures and religions consider certain species or even individual trees as sacred, and to walk in a summer woodland it is very easy to understand why.

Butterflies & Moths

We often associate butterflies and moths with flowers and open grassland, but there are lots of species that thrive among the trees. Here are some that live among our old oak tree.

Great Purple Hairstreak

Great Purple Hairstreak Eggs

The **great purple hairstreak** is a small butterfly that is dependent on oak trees through all stages of its life. It feeds on a substance called honeydew, which is secreted by aphids onto the leaves of the tree, and it lays its eggs at the base of the leaf bud.

The caterpillars do not emerge until the following spring, when they spin tiny silk webs, which catch debris and form excellent camouflage. The pupa (chrysalis) can produce a squeak that may attract ants. The ants then take the pupa into their nests where it remains safe until the adult butterfly emerges.

The **American oak beauty** is one of many moth species whose caterpillars feed only on oak leaves. The adult moths are mottled gray to camouflage themselves against the bark of the tree, while the caterpillars, when still, appear just like tiny twigs.

The **peppered moth** also relies on camouflage to hide against the bark of trees. In the nineteenth century, during the height of the British Industrial Revolution, it evolved to be much darker as the trees were blackened by pollution.

In **Africa**, some cultures believe that if a butterfly comes into your home, it is the spirit of an ancestor and shouldn't be disturbed.

A similar belief occurred across much of Europe and Asia, where butterflies were believed to be either the souls of the dead or guardians who would guide souls on to the afterlife.

Fledglings

Having carefully built their nests in secret places among the trees, many birds hatch their eggs to coincide with the abundance of moth and butterfly caterpillars, which they feed their chicks with.

Songbirds

Through early spring, the forest is filled with birdsong, but by the arrival of the summer solstice, most of the songs will have ceased, and instead the trees fill with quiet peeps and weak contact calls between parent birds and their young. The fledglings must quickly learn to be quiet and discreet, which isn't easy when they have learned to beg for food in the nest.

Birds of Prey

Birds of prey time their nesting to coincide with the appearance of vulnerable, smaller fledglings. It might seem sad, but the hawks have their own young to feed, and the young birds that learn to be stealthy and dodge capture will one day be able to teach their own young how best to survive. In a healthy forest, everything exists in balance.

Bats

Bats cannot bore holes of their own but use crevices and cracks, perhaps created after strong winds or a lightning strike, or cavities formed by decay. They will also tuck themselves behind ivy where they can hang up their feet and stay safely out of sight until night falls.

Creatures of the Night

Most bats are nocturnal and hunt and fly by using echolocation. They make a series of high frequency sounds that bounce back off objects or prey species like moths. Bats have incredible hearing that enable them to pick up the sound of the echoes and then know precisely where things are.

Supernatural Bats

Because they often don't emerge until it is dark and then appear from seemingly nowhere, bats have long been associated with the supernatural. In ancient Greece they were associated with the underworld, while the Celts believed they were mischievous spirits who could cross the veil between worlds. This is why they are often associated with Halloween, or depicted as a witch's familiar.

Gall Ink

The oak tree's fertilized female flowers will be beginning to develop into acorns. They will be small, green, and difficult to see. More conspicuous might be small, round, green balls called oak apples. They are actually galls, and are not formed by the tree itself.

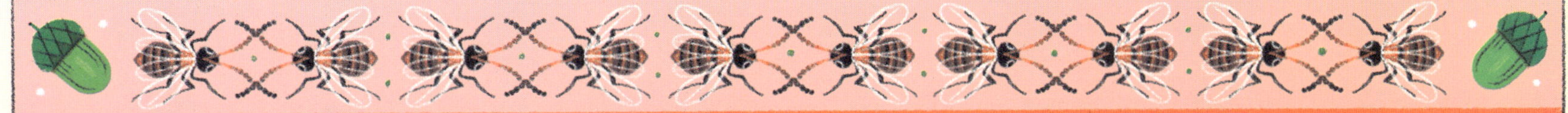

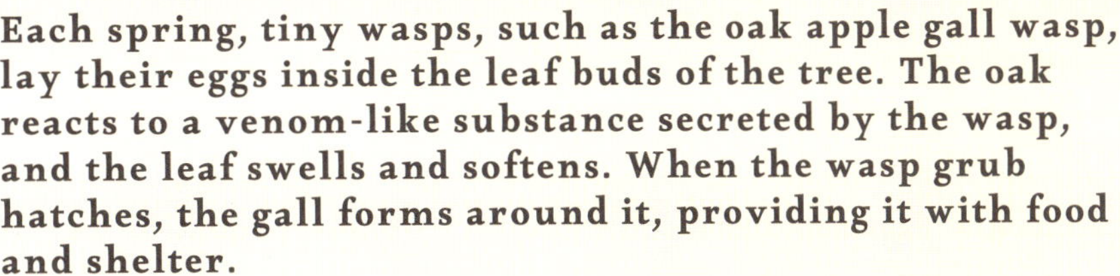

Each spring, tiny wasps, such as the oak apple gall wasp, lay their eggs inside the leaf buds of the tree. The oak reacts to a venom-like substance secreted by the wasp, and the leaf swells and softens. When the wasp grub hatches, the gall forms around it, providing it with food and shelter.

The galls harden over time, and in the late summer and early autumn, they can be collected to make ink and dye. Galls contain high levels of tannin, which is also found in the bark of the tree, and since Roman times they have been used to make iron gall ink. Many historic documents, including the Declaration of Independence, were written with iron gall ink.

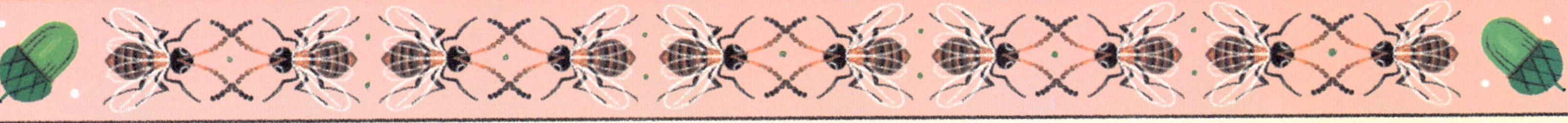

Green Man

I like to walk in the woods in the summer and try to remember how stark and bare it looked in the winter.

The contrast could not be greater, and the trees that six months ago stood bare-branched are now lush and vibrant in full leaf. This extraordinary regeneration has long fascinated people and inspired a lot of imagery and symbolism across cultures.

The Green Man is a figure or face covered in leaves and moss with possible roots in Celtic or Roman folklore.

He became a representation of regrowth and often features in carvings or stonework on churches, cathedrals, and Gothic architecture.

People often wear costumes or masks to represent the Green Man in festivals or parades named after him.

Woodwose

The Woodwose was a wild man of the woods and a widespread figure in medieval European folklore. He was said to be naked but covered in long hair, and seemed to be representative of primitive existence, hunting food and living among the trees. Various Woodwose depictions have appeared in art, heraldry, and literature, representations that suggest an unknown, mythical quality rather than something or someone to fear.

Litha

The ancient Celts celebrated the solstice with the festival of Litha, during which they lit ceremonial bonfires, also known as St. John's Fires, which would purify the landscape and protect crops and livestock.

Leaf-covered "Green Men" who triumph to bring life over death can be discovered all over the world. Across Europe—in France, Spain, and the Netherlands—and as far away as India, images appear in sculptures and artwork.

THE AUTUMN EQUINOX

Wrap up warm as we wander out in the autumn air.

As summer drifts toward autumn, the air softens and the days shorten, before once again we reach the moment when nighttime matches the length of the day. The autumn equinox comes as the tilt of the earth allows the sun to illuminate the Northern and Southern Hemispheres equally.

With less sunlight, the chlorophyll in our oak tree is no longer able to bring green to the leaves, which instead change color to red, orange, or yellow and then to brown. The acorns are also beginning to brown and as they ripen, they drop from their cups. On the ground they might be eaten by boar and deer or collected by squirrels and birds.

Thunder

Due to its often-solitary nature and high-water content, the oak tree is prone to lightning strikes. Because of this, many cultures believed that the oak could protect against thunder, and it was revered as a result. In Norse mythology, the god Thor had a strong association with the oak tree. He wielded a giant hammer called Mjölnir, which some people believed could create lightning, while the sound of thunder came from the great chariot he rode across the sky.

New Life

Acorns have long been seen as a symbol of fertility. The Celts believed that they could bring good fortune and prosperity and that if a bridegroom placed one in their pocket on their wedding day, then it would bless the union.

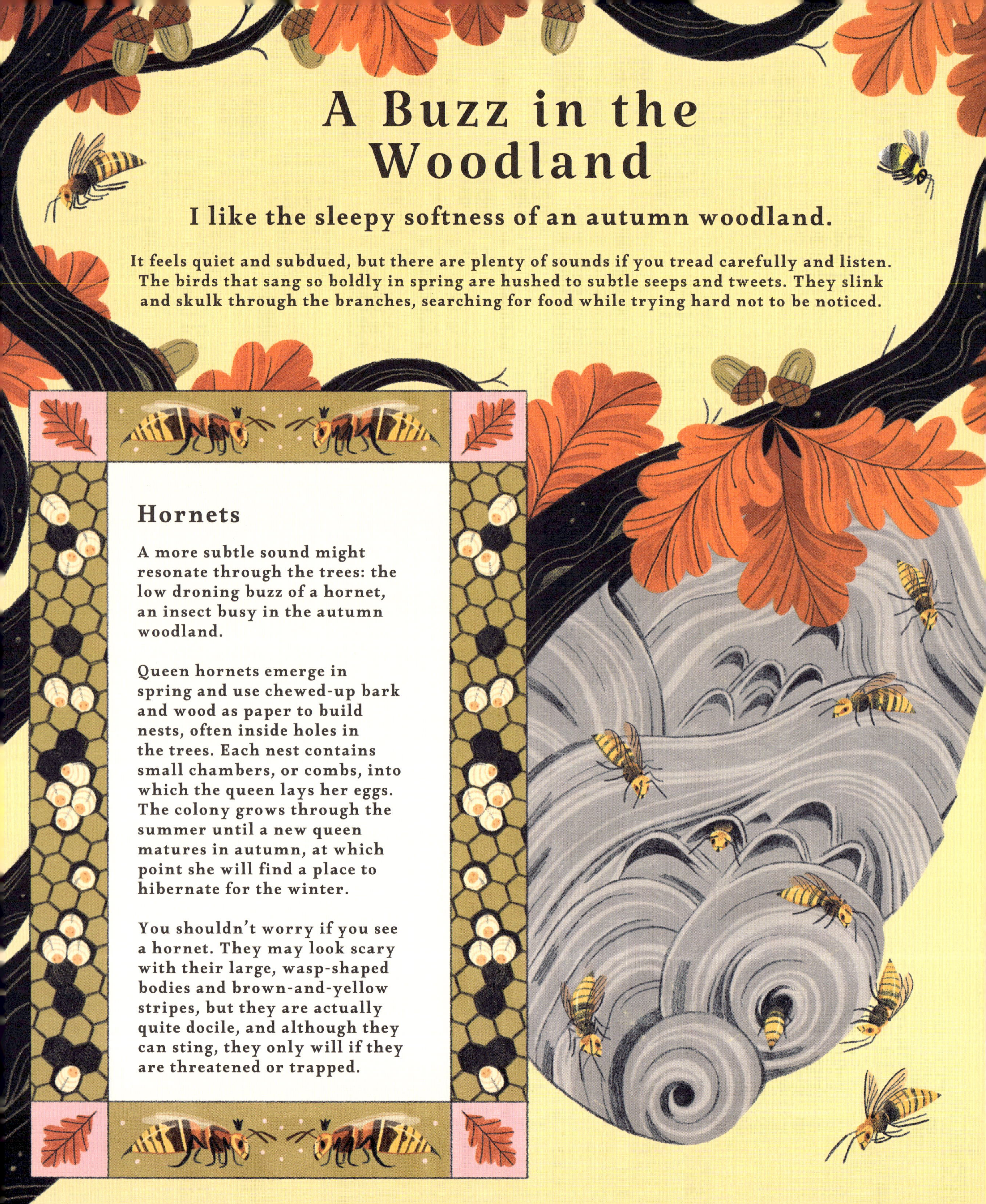

A Buzz in the Woodland

I like the sleepy softness of an autumn woodland.

It feels quiet and subdued, but there are plenty of sounds if you tread carefully and listen. The birds that sang so boldly in spring are hushed to subtle seeps and tweets. They slink and skulk through the branches, searching for food while trying hard not to be noticed.

Hornets

A more subtle sound might resonate through the trees: the low droning buzz of a hornet, an insect busy in the autumn woodland.

Queen hornets emerge in spring and use chewed-up bark and wood as paper to build nests, often inside holes in the trees. Each nest contains small chambers, or combs, into which the queen lays her eggs. The colony grows through the summer until a new queen matures in autumn, at which point she will find a place to hibernate for the winter.

You shouldn't worry if you see a hornet. They may look scary with their large, wasp-shaped bodies and brown-and-yellow stripes, but they are actually quite docile, and although they can sting, they only will if they are threatened or trapped.

Bumblebees

Bumblebees are similarly passive and also apparent in an autumn woodland. They, too, build nests in trees, but also use holes in the ground, especially around exposed roots or inside old rodent burrows.

In autumn, the new queens and fertile males leave their nests. They mate before the males die and the fertilized queens hibernate before beginning the nest-building process in spring.

On sunny winter days the queens might stir and look for food. This is why plants such as snowdrops, which may flower in winter, and early-appearing springtime flowers are so important. They provide nectar when there is very little food around.

Dumbledores

In folklore, people believed that a bumblebee flying around your window signified the arrival of an unexpected guest.

In Old English, bumblebees were known as "dumbledores," a name familiar today as a wizarding headmaster from the Harry Potter tales.

Fungi

In the autumn, fruiting bodies poke up above the earth. These are fungi—mushrooms and toadstools—and come in all sorts of different shapes and sizes.

Fairy Rings

Some mushrooms grow in rings that were long believed to be the work of fairies or other mythical creatures. In Austria, it was said that the rings were created by the tails of dragons, while in Germany they were called Hexenringe (witch rings) and marked the spot where witches danced.

Friend or Foe?

Some fungi, like the cep (or porcini) and chanterelle, are highly prized as food, but other species such as the death cap can be deadly poisonous. I have learned to identify many of the woodland mushrooms and will never touch one unless I know its name.

In some cultures, mushrooms would be used for medicine or ritual. Fly agaric was used for killing flies. Today we are more likely to see the distinctive red-and-white mushroom in paintings, fairy tales, and even video games like Super Mario Bros.

Connected Forest

Within the surface layers of the forest floor are networks of thin strands known as mycelium. The threads look like tiny roots and can spread across huge areas, forming a network that can link different trees together, allowing one tree to exchange resources with another. The forest truly is a remarkable, singular entity.

The largest known colony is of a honey fungus in the Blue Mountains in Oregon, which covers some 3.5 square miles (9 sq. km). It is over two thousand years old and may be the largest single living thing in the world.

The mycelium helps break down the leaf litter and adds nutrients to the soil. It takes carbon from the trees while giving nitrogen in return.

Berries, Nuts & Hips

Across the forest, the colors are fading.

The bright, vibrant greens of spring and summer change into the soft yellows and rust-browns of autumn. But the colors can look beautiful at this time of year, and even when the leaves fall, bright beads of berries and rose hips may remain.

Hazelnut trees produce nuts that have a hard shell to protect the softer seed within.

The horse chestnut protects its seeds in spiked, spherical cases.

The fruit of elder and dogwood form as small, black berries that occur in clusters.

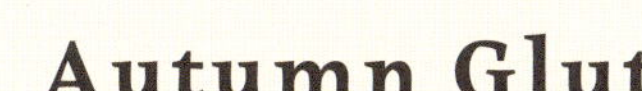

Autumn Glut

A gentle drift through a weakening sun before the harsh cold of winter . . . A time when much of the fruit and food that the plants have strived to produce is ripe and ready . . . This is sometimes called "autumn glut."

Beware the Berry

Some berries might be edible for people, but many are poisonous. The yew, for example, produces soft, bright red arils, which are edible, while the seeds within are deadly poisonous; a bird's digestive system might allow the seed to pass intact without any ill effect, but mammals (such as people) are likely to ingest the poison and become very sick.

Birds of a Feather

Some species, such as waxwings, flock together in winter and gorge on berries. They stay together for safety and will often remain in a single group of trees until all the berries have been eaten. As they move around, they disperse the seeds into different areas, helping the trees to spread.

In his ode "To Autumn," the poet John Keats called this time:

"Season of mists and mellow fruitfulness,
Close bosom-friend of the maturing sun."

Owls

As dusk falls in the forest, different creatures begin to stir.

Deer, rodents, and boar will move more confidently in the dark. Bats flit among the branches, and owls begin to call. Woodland species of owls are often at their most vocal in autumn as they begin to form territories and attempt to attract a mate.

Owls have enormous eyeballs which collect more light in dusky conditions, allowing them to see better in the dark. Their eyes are fixed in place, so in order to look around they have to move their head through 270 degrees.

Ghostly Quiet

The feathers of an owl have serrated edges that diffuse the air as it passes across them. This hinders speed, but enables them to fly in near silence, a much more valuable attribute when hunting in the dusk and dark. This silent flight has prompted them to be mistaken as ghosts, especially if they are seen flying in low light over graveyards or forest edges.

Ominous Owls

In Japan, owls are thought to be lucky and to provide protection from suffering, while in Indian folklore they represent wisdom and prescience. The ancient Greeks also believed owls to be wise, possibly because little owls would nest upon the architraves of temples and look down upon people in the manner of the gods themselves. This inspired the little owl's Latin name, *Athene noctua*, taken from Athena, the goddess of wisdom.

THE WINTER SOLSTICE

Just as the summer solstice brought us the longest day of the year, so the winter solstice marks the longest night.

Under clear skies and the silver sparkle of the moon and stars, the temperature will tumble, bringing crisp frosts and icy dawns.

During the day, the sun slips across the sky on a shallow arc, too low for its weakened warmth to reach much of the landscape. There, within the shade, the ground may remain frozen and snow unthawed.

New buds dot the bare branches of our oak, waiting for spring, protecting themselves from the cold with overlapping scales.

Despite the chill and lack of daylight, the winter solstice has long been a time for celebration, marking the rebirth of the sun, or used as an opportunity to meet with family and friends before the weather worsens.

Undercover

As an oak tree ages, its bark darkens and thickens. It begins to look like the skin of a crocodile, with furrows and grooves inside which invertebrates can hide. In the winter, lots of animals will use the oak tree to hibernate, but we shall peek at them shortly.

Tannin

If the bark is split or broken, then the tree will release tannin, which acts as a natural preservative. This is the substance that is found in the wasp galls and used to make ink. Oak tannin has also long been used to preserve leather, hence the process known as tanning.

Other Worlds

The word *duir* was used in several ancient languages to describe both an oak tree and a door, suggesting the belief in a connection between the two was shared across many cultures. The Celts believed oak trees to be gateways to wisdom and knowledge. It was also believed that should you fall asleep beneath an oak tree, you might wake in another world.

Mistletoe

Although deciduous trees drop their own leaves in winter, they may carry the green of other plants upon their frame.

The trunks and lower branches might be clad in ivy, hugging tightly like a winter coat. Higher up, often in the branches of the crown, you might spot balls of mistletoe.

Mistletoe is a parasitic plant that takes water and nutrients from the tree on which it grows. It is evergreen, with stiff stems and pairs of leathery green leaves. The seeds are contained within white berries that appear through the winter. The berries are poisonous, but some birds, such as the mistle thrush can tolerate the toxin and feed upon them.

The fleshy part of the berry contains a glue-like substance called viscin, which can stick the seeds to the beaks of feeding birds. When the birds wipe their beaks clean on another branch, the seeds drop off, allowing new mistletoe to grow.

Druids would collect mistletoe at specific points within the lunar cycle, believing its powers to be in rhythm with those of the moon. Those properties would be strengthened further if the mistletoe was cut from the tree with a sickle made of gold.
Celts believed that mistletoe had supernatural qualities, derived from the thunder god Taranis, that enabled it to survive through the winter.
In Pagan tradition, mistletoe berries were linked to male fertility.
Romans would hang mistletoe above doorways to bring blessings of peace and love.
In Greek mythology, it was said that a sprig of mistletoe could grant access to the underworld.
In Christian culture, mistletoe has been used as a decoration with which to ward off witches and demons. There is also an enduring tradition to kiss beneath it, and in some places you must remove a berry each time you do.

Hibernation

The short, cold days and lack of food mean winter can be punishing for wildlife. Different species adopt different methods in order to cope.

Some mammals will hibernate. They lower their metabolic rates and body temperatures and slip into a state similar to deep sleep. If they have eaten sufficient food in the autumn to sustain theselves, and so long as they remain undisturbed, they will not wake until spring.

Bears

One large mammal known for residing in caves is the brown bear, who may also dig dens within the soil. Bears do not fully hibernate but will instead wake from time to time and forage for food.

Migration

Many birds will migrate, some flying thousands of miles to warmer climes, while those that remain might form large flocks and use one another's body heat to keep warm as they roost.

Hornets and Bees

Many insects, such as the hornets and bumblebees that we saw in autumn, will die off in winter, with just the pregnant queens hibernating until spring.

Butterflies and Moths

Butterflies and moths hibernate in many different ways, either as eggs or pupa, as caterpillars in spun silk nests or as adults in crevices and cracks in trees.

The comma has slightly ragged, scalloped wings with flecked brown and pale colors on the underwings. When closed, they look like dead leaves, enabling the adults to camouflage themselves as such in order to hibernate through the winter.

Small Mammals

One small mammal that hibernates is the meadow jumping mouse. They may remain tucked away for up to seven or eight months in underground burrows where they nestle in nests made from grass or leaves.

Hedgehogs and Bats

Hedgehogs also build nests from vegetation and coil themselves up inside to hibernate, while bats may use holes in trees, such as the oak, or in old buildings and caves.

Tree Blessings

Though we have long made use of trees and wood for building, fuel, and food, we do not respect them today quite as we once did.

Many ancient cultures would offer thanks and blessings to the trees, to ensure healthy growth and give gratitude for all that they provide.

Cedar Blessing

Many indigenous people in the Pacific Northwest, especially those in British Columbia, Canada, honor the cedar tree. The cedar is traditionally used in medicine and for a wide range of purposes, with all parts of the tree utilized. The roots are used to make hats and baskets, while the smaller branches are used to make rope and weapons. The outer bark can be made into armor, and the softer, fibrous material inside used for bedding. Before a tree is harvested, it is traditionally offered a blessing, and its parts are removed in a way that makes sure it will survive.

Oak Prophecies

Oak trees have often been a source of worship or blessing. At the oracle of Dodona in ancient Greece, priests and priestesses were said to study the sound and movement of a sacred oak tree to make prophecies.

Sacred Fig

In the Indian subcontinent, widespread reverence is paid to the sacred fig. The tree was venerated during the Bronze Age by Indus Valley civilizations and has since played a significant role in Hinduism, Sikhism, Jainism, and Buddhism. The Bodhi Tree, beneath which Siddhartha Gautama, the Buddha, found enlightenment, was a sacred fig, and its heart-shaped leaves are often used within religious symbolism.

Wassailing

A long-held European tradition is known as wassailing, taken from the Norse *waes hael* which means "be healthy." It took many forms, but was essentially a blessing and celebration that took place around the New Year. In some areas, such as southwestern England, the practice evolved to bless apple trees in order to ensure a fine harvest (and finer cider!) in the forthcoming year.

Winter Woodlore

Tree blessings are not all made within the forest.

For thousands of years, people have attempted to harness the power of woodlore, to bring fortune and good health to homes and our loved ones.

Wreaths

In ancient Egyptian, Chinese, and Hebrew cultures, evergreen trees were seen as symbolic of eternal life. Wreaths and garlands would be made from leaves and branches, then hung as decorations or worn on the body. The Greek god Apollo was depicted as wearing a wreath of laurel upon his head, a practice adopted by Roman emperors, such as Julius Caesar, for whom the wreaths represented victory and honor.

Yule Logs

In Europe, particularly among the Germanic peoples, a winter festival of singing and feasting called Yule would take place.

Part of these traditions would be the burning of a yule log, a piece of wood, perhaps decorated in fruit and leaves, that would be set alight to bring good health and protection.

This endures to this day, although many yule logs are now made from cake and chocolate and eaten rather than burned. Yule, like many other winter celebrations, has become incorporated into the Christian festival of Christmas, which marks the birth of Jesus. Sprigs of holly and ivy may be hung from beams and mantelpieces, while evergreen wreaths are often hung from doors.

Christmas Trees

Most familiar today is the Christmas Tree.

A spruce, pine, or fir is brought into many Christian homes for the holiday season. The tree is adorned with ornaments, a star or angel is placed at the top of the tree, strands of lights sparkle among the needles, and gifts for family and friends are placed beneath.

Holly

Pagans believed that holly could bring protection from evil spirits, and would wear small sprigs in their hair.

Originally given as a gift during the Roman winter festival of Saturnalia, holly was later adopted by Christians as a representation of the crown of thorns that Jesus wore before his crucifixion, with the red berries symbolizing his blood.

Glossary

Architrave – A beam or frame around a door or on top of columns in buildings

Aril – A juicy or colorful part around a seed, like the red covering on a pomegranate seed

Beltane – An old springtime festival from Scotland and Ireland, with bonfires and dancing

Bridegroom – A man who is getting married

Bud – A small bump on a plant that can grow into a leaf, flower, or branch

Camouflage – Colors or patterns that help animals hide in their surroundings

Celt / Celtic – People from parts of Europe including Ireland, Scotland, Wales, Cornwall, and Brittany

Christian – Someone who believes in Jesus Christ and follows the teachings of the Bible

Contact call – A sound animals make to stay in touch with their babies

Crucifix – A cross; also an important Christian symbol

Deciduous – Trees that lose their leaves in the autumn, like maples and oaks

Dumbledore – An old word for a bumblebee

Echolocation – A way animals like bats map out their surroundings with sound, by listening to echoes

Enlightenment – A moment when someone understands something very deeply

Equinox – A day when there are 12 hours of daylight and 12 hours of night, which happens twice a year

Fertility – The ability to grow new life, like plants making seeds or animals having babies

Fertilized – When a seed or egg starts to grow

Fledgling – A baby bird that has grown feathers and is learning to fly

Folklore – Old stories and traditions passed down through families and cultures

Forage – To search for food in nature

Fungi – Living things like mushrooms that grow from rotting materials

Gall – A little lump that grows on plants, often made by bugs

Glut – Having far too much of something

Gothic – A style of art, buildings, or stories that are dark, spooky, and dramatic

Green Man – A face made of leaves, showing nature's power and spirit

Habitat – The natural home where an animal or plant lives

Hibernate – What some animals do to survive winter: They rest or are inactive for a long time.

Indigenous people – The first people to live in a place

Leaf litter – Old leaves on the ground that help feed the forest

Lichen – A mix of fungus and algae that grows on rocks and trees

Litha – A summer holiday celebrated on the longest day of the year

Lunar cycle – The changing shapes of the moon, from new to full and back again

May Day – A spring celebration on May 1 with flowers and dancing

Mjölnir – Thor's magical hammer in Norse myths; He used it to protect people.

Monoecious – A plant that has both male and female parts, so it can make seeds by itself

Mycelia – Tiny threads that grow underground and help fungi spread

Mythology – Old stories about gods, heroes, and magical creatures from different cultures

Needfire – A special fire thought to bring good luck and keep away bad things

Norse – People from ancient Scandinavia (like Vikings), with their own myths and legends

Northern Hemisphere – The top half of Earth, above the equator

Ominous – A word for when it seems something may be about to happen, especially something scary or bad

Pagan – A person who believes in nature and old gods instead of modern religions

Parasitic – Living on another plant or animal and taking its nutrients

Preservative – Something that helps food or other things stay fresh longer

Prophecy – A message or story that tells what might happen in the future

Rose hip – The fruit of a rose plant; it holds the seeds and is often red or orange.

Sapling – A young tree

Serrated – Edges with little points, like a saw or some leaves

Solstice – The longest or shortest day of the year, when the sun is at its highest or lowest

Southern Hemisphere – The bottom half of Earth, below the equator

Supernatural – Things that are magical or can't be explained by science

Tannin – A bitter part in some plants that helps protect them (like in acorns or tea leaves)

Understory – The layer of small plants and trees that grow under big forest trees

Underworld – A place where spirits or the dead live in myths and legends

Viscin – A super sticky substance from seeds that helps them stick to things (like bird beaks)

Wassailing – Singing and cheering to wish good luck

Woodwose – A wild man from old forest stories, like a forest giant

Wreath – A circle made of flowers or leaves, often hung on doors for holidays

Yule – An old winter festival that is now part of Christmas celebrations

To Jenny—for finding the path through the trees. —K.P.

To all the wild folk, the weirdos and fools, the trailblazers, the faeries and dragons and witches, to all my dancers and dreamers—stand tall, stay magical. —A.S.

The illustrations in this book were created digitally.
Set in Alkalami, Bloom, Gowun, Katibeh, and Wigwams.

Library of Congress Control Number 2025942633
ISBN 978-1-4197-8670-9

Book design by Nicola Price

Printed and bound in China
10 9 8 7 6 5 4 3 2 1

ABRAMS The Art of Books
195 Broadway, New York, NY 10007
abramsbooks.com